GOOD SHIP LOLLIPOP
AND OTHER FUN SONGS TO SING AND PLAY

Edited and Produced by John L. Haag

CONTENTS

This publication ©1996 Creative Concepts Publishing Corporation
Printed in the U.S.A.   All Rights Reserved

Catalog #07-1076
ISBN# 1-56922-104-9

Exclusive Distributor for
CREATIVE CONCEPTS PUBLISHING CORP.
2290 Eastman Avenue #110, Ventura, California 93003

10.95

ON THE GOOD SHIP LOLLIPOP

Words and Music by Sidney Clare and Richard A. Whiting

2

4

I CAN SEE CLEARLY NOW

Words and Music by Johnny Nash

6

ALEXANDER'S RAGTIME BAND

Words and Music by Irving Berlin

land,............ They can play a bu – gle call like you nev – er heard be-fore,

So nat – ur – al that you want to go to war; That's just the

best – est band what am, hon – ey lamb, Come on a –

long,............... Come on a – long,............... Let me take you by the

ABA DABA HONEYMOON

Words and Music by Arthur Fields and Walter Donovan

ALLEY-OOP

Words and Music by Dallas Frazier

AMERICA, I LOVE YOU

Words by Edgar Leslie
Music by Archie Gottler

19

BALLIN' THE JACK

Words by Jim Burris
Music by Chris Smith

Folks in Geor-gia's
It's being done at

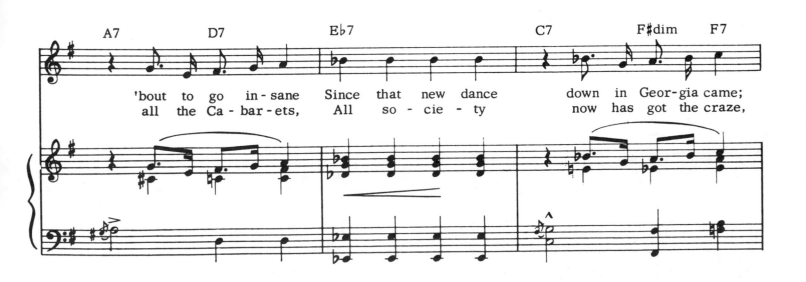

'bout to go in-sane, Since that new dance down in Geor-gia came;
all the Ca-bar-ets, All so-cie-ty now has got the craze,

Chorus *(not too fast)*

First you put your two knees close up tight,— Then you

sway 'em to the left, then you sway 'em to the right,

Step a - round the floor kind of nice and light,— Then you

twis' a - round and twis' a - round with all — your might,—

BATTLE OF NEW ORLEANS

Words by Jimmy Driftwood
Music by Johnny Horton

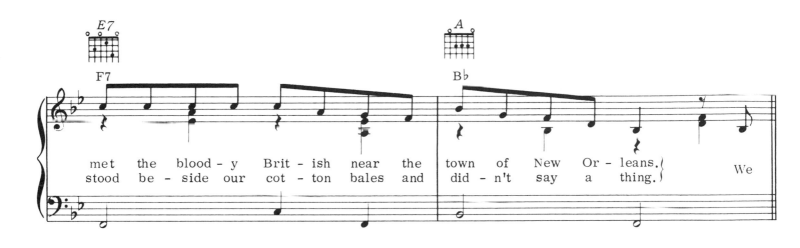

met the blood-y Brit-ish near the town of New Or-leans.
stood be-side our cot-ton bales and did-n't say a thing.

We

Chorus

fired our guns and the Brit-ish kept a-com-in', There wuz-n't nigh as man-y as they

wuz a while a-go. We fired once more and they be-gan to run-nin', On

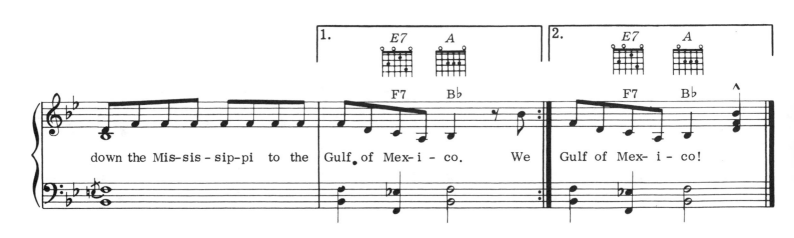

down the Mis-sis-sip-pi to the Gulf of Mex-i-co. We

Gulf of Mex-i-co!

THE CANDY MAN

Words and Music by Leslie Bricusse and Anthony Newley

Moderato, joyfully

Who can take a sun - rise sprin - kle it with dew,
Who can take a rain - bow wrap it in a sigh,

cov - er it in choc -'late and a mir - a - cle or two? The
soak it in the sun and make a straw -b'ry lem - on pie?

can - dy man, (The can - dy man, the can - dy man can. the

28

CASEY JONES (The Brave Engineer)

Words by T. Lawrence Seibert
Music by Eddie Newton

THE CAT CAME BACK

Arranged and Adapted by John L. Haag

ver - y next day, The cat came back, they thought he was a gon - er but the

cat came back, It just could-n't stay a - way.

The man around the corner swore he'd kill the cat on sight,
He loaded up his shotgun with nails and dynamite;
He waited and he waited for the cat to come around,
Ninety-seven pieces of the man is all they found.

He gave it to a little boy with a dollar note,
Told him for to take it up the river in a boat;
They tied a rope around its neck, it must have weighed a pound,
Now they drag the river for a little boy that's drowned.

He gave it to a man going up in a balloon,
He told him for to take it to the man in the moon,
The balloon came down about ninety miles away,
Where he is now, well I dare not say.

He gave it to a man going way out west,
Told him for to take it to the one he loved the best;
First the train hit the curve, then it jumped the rail,
Not a soul was left behind to tell the gruesome tale.

The cat it had some company one night out in the yard,
Someone threw a boot-jack, and they threw it mighty hard,
It caught the cat behind the ear, she thought it rather slight,
When along came a brick-bat and knocked the cat out of sight.

Away across the ocean they did send the cat at last,
Vessel only out a day and making the water fast;
People all began to pray, the boat began to toss,
A great big gust of wind came by and every soul was lost.

On a telegraph wire, sparrows sitting in a bunch,
The cat was feeling hungry, thought she'd like 'em for a lunch;
Climbing softly up the pole, and when she reached the top,
Put her foot upon the electric wire, which tied her in a knot.

DIXIE

Words and Music by Dan Emmet

DON'T SIT UNDER THE APPLE TREE

Words and Music by Charles Tobias, Lew Brown and Sam H. Stept

EVERYTHING IS BEAUTIFUL

Words and Music by Ray Stevens

Moderately

Je - sus loves the lit - tle chil - dren, all the lit - tle chil - dren of the world, Red and yel - low, black and white, they are pre - cious in His sight, Je - sus loves the lit - tle chil - dren of the world._____

CHORUS

Eve - ry -thing is Beau - ti - ful_____ in its own way,_____ Like a star - ry

Verse 2: We shouldn't care about the length of his hair or the color of his skin
Don't worry about what shows from without but the love that lives within
We gonna get it all together now and everything gonna work out fine
Just take a little time to look on the good side my friend and straighten it out in your mind.

HAIL, HAIL, THE GANG'S ALL HERE

Arranged and Adapted by John L. Haag

Hail! Hail! The gang's all here, What the heck do we care, What the heck do we care. Hail! Hail! The gang's all here, What the heck do we care now!

GIVE MY REGARD TO BROADWAY

Words and Music by George M. Cohan

I'M FOREVER BLOWING BUBBLES

Words and Music by Jaan Kenbrovin and John W. Kellette

ITSY BITSY TEENIE WEENIE YELLOW POLKADOT BIKINI

Words and Music by Lee Pockriss and Paul J. Vance

JAVA JIVE

Words by Milton Drake
Music by Ben Oakland

Lightly, with an easy beat

LONG TALL TEXAN

Words and Music by Henry Strzelecki

With a steady beat

Gid-dy up,   Gid-dy up,   Well I'm a

1. LONG TALL TEX-AN_____ I ride a big ____ white ___ horse (He rides from
2. LONG TALL TEX-AN_____ I wear a ten ____ gal-lon hat (He rides from
3. LONG TALL TEX-AN_____ I en-force jus-tice for the law (He rides from

Tex-as on a big___ white ___ horse) Yes I'm a LONG ____ TALL ___ TEX-AN ____
Tex-as with a ten ___ gallon hat) Yes I'm a LONG ___ TALL ___ TEX-AN ____
Tex-as to en-force ___ the ___ law) Yes I'm a LONG ___ TALL ___ TEX-AN ____

MAIRZY DOATS

Words and Music by Milton Drake, Al Hoffman and Jerry Livingston

THE NAME GAME

Words and Music by Shirley Elliston and Lincoln Chase

63

OH, JOHNNY, OH!

Words by Ed Rose
Music by Abe Olman

Moderately bright

Verse

All the girls are cra-zy 'bout a cer-tain lit-tle lad,___ Al-tho' he's

ver-y, ver-y bad,___ He could be, oh so good when he want-ed to.

Bad or good he un-der-stood 'bout love and oth-er things,___ For ev-'ry

PEANUT BUTTER

Words and Music by Smith, Goldsmith, Barnum and Cooper

PINK SHOE LACES

Words and Music by Mickey Grant

CHORUS

1. He wears
2. He's got
3. He want-ed
4. With my

Tan shoes with PINK SHOE LAC-ES, A pol-ka dot vest and man, Oh, man. He wears

He's got
He want-ed
With my

Tan shoes with PINK SHOE LAC-ES and a big pan-a-ma with a pur-ple hat band.

1.

To Verse 2.

2. He
3. Now
4. Now

And a big pan-a-ma with a pur-ple hat band.

THE PURPLE PEOPLE EATER

Words and Music by Sheb Wooley

Bright rock tempo

Verse:

G

1. Well, I saw the thing__ a - com - in' out of the sky, __ It had
2. (Well, he) came down to earth__ and he lit in a tree, __ I said,

D7   G   G7

one long horn and one big eye. __   I com-menced to shak - in' and I
"Mis - ter Pur - ple Peo - ple Eat - er, don't eat me." __   I heard him say in a

QUE SERA, SERA (Whatever Will Be, Will Be)

Words and Music by Jay Livingston and Ray Evans

RAGTIME COWBOY JOE

Words by Grant Clarke
Music by Lewis F. Muir and Maurice Abrahams

SCHOOL DAYS (When We Were A Couple Of Kids)

Words by Will D. Cobb
Music by Gus Edwards

ROCK-A-BYE YOUR BABY WITH A DIXIE MELODY

Words by Sam M. Lewis and Joe Young
Music by Jean Schwartz

SHOO FLY PIE AND APPLE PAN DOWDY

Words by Sammy Gallop
Music by Guy Wood

Slow bounce

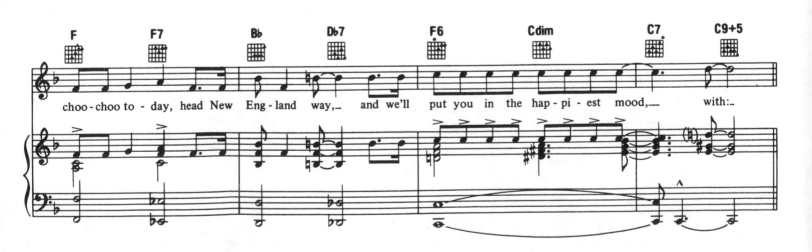

TOO-RA-LOO-RA-LOO-RAL (That's An Irish Lullaby)

Words and Music by J. R. Shannon

TAKE ME OUT TO THE BALL GAME

Words by Jack Norworth
Music by Albert von Tilzer

THE TEDDY BEAR'S PICNIC

Words and Music by John W. Bratton and James B. Kennedy

1. you go down in the woods to-day You're sure of a big sur-prise.___ If
2. Ev'-ry Ted-dy Bear who's been good Is sure of a treat to-day.___ There's

you go down in the woods to-day You'd bet-ter go in dis-guise;___ For
lots of mar-vel-ous things to eat, And won-der-ful games to play.___ Be-

ev'- ry Bear that ev - er there was Will gath - er there for cer-tain, be-cause To-
neath the trees where no-bod-y sees They'll Hide and Seek as long as they please,'Cause

day's the day the Ted-dy Bears have their Pic - nic.
that's the way the Ted-dy Bears have their Pic - nic.

INTERLUDE

VOICE

If you go down in the woods to-day You'd bet-ter not go a - lone.___ It's

96

WAITING FOR THE ROBERT E. LEE

Words by L. Wolfe Gilbert
Music by Lewis F. Muir

D.S.

WHEN IRISH EYES ARE SMILING

Words by Chauncey Olcott and Geo. Graff, Jr.
Music by Ernest R. Ball

Moderately

WHEN YOU'RE SMILING

Words and Music by Mark Fisher, Joe Goodwin and Larry Shay

I'M ALWAYS CHASING RAINBOWS

Words by Joseph McCarthy
Music by Harry Carroll

TAMMY

Words and Music by Jay Livingston and Ray Evans

I'D LIKE TO TEACH THE WORLD TO SING

Words and Music by B. Backer, B. Davis, R. Cook and R. Greenaway

I'd like to build the world a home and fur-nish it with love,

Grow ap-ple trees and hon-ey bees and

snow-white tur-tle doves. I'd like to teach the world

to sing in per-fect har-mo-ny, I'd